100 Days of Mindfulness:
HEART

100 Days of Mindfulness:
HEART

A JOURNAL

Tracey Moore Lukkarila

ISBN 978-1-54397-862-9

Mandala artwork and book design by
Tracey Moore Lukkarila

We don't have to go anywhere
to obtain the truth.
We only need to be still and
things will reveal themselves
in the clear water of our heart.

--Thich Nhat Hanh, "Moments of Mindfulness"

Contents

Preface

In 2014, I broke mentally and spiritually. It was a horrific time for me. My depression was so severe I wasn't sure I could make it back. Through hard work and lots of journaling, I did indeed find my way back.

My journey has been one of self-exploration. Mindfulness has been my #1 tool for staying sane. Through mindfulness, I have learned to manage my thoughts and emotions, and stay focused on what's important in life.

Journaling has been important to my recovery and growth, keeping me accountable to the work of maintaining sanity. Over the years, I bought dozens of journals but none fit what I needed. I wanted something simple that kept me focused on mindfulness, so I developed my own. In 2016, I published "100 Days of Mindfulness: Presence" journal based on my personal journey. "Presence" reflected my mindfulness practice at that time; focused on getting present through awareness of sensation, breath, and thought.

I didn't know what the next theme would be, or if I'd publish another journal. But in the past year, I've become curious about mindfulness of my heart and began creating exercises focused on tuning into my heart physically, emotionally, and spiritually. This "Heart" journal contains a selection of the mindfulness exercises I've used to dig deeper inside myself to discover what's really in my heart. It's been an incredible journey of discovering who I am and who I really want to be.

I invite you on a journey of your heart. I hope you find this heart-focused journal as enlightening as I have.

--Tracey Moore Lukkarila, July 2019

 # Acknowledgments

The heart takes up physical space in our body, so we can sense its presence. We can feel it pumping and pulsing blood. Our heart is a concept as well. It's where we imagine love exists and we feel physical aching when our "heart is broken." We "search our heart" to find our true feelings, desires, and intention. We "do what's in our heart" to feel at one with ourselves and our world.

I became fascinated with this as I grew in my practice as a Baptiste yoga student and teacher. Baptiste yoga instructors talk about the heart in every class. We are told to open up our chest space to create an open heart. We place our hands on our chest and express gratitude for our heart. We are challenged to spend time being in stillness with our hearts.

It's a powerful practice. I began to incorporate these concepts into my mindfulness exercises for use off the yoga mat. With them I'm able to sustain feelings of gratitude, empowerment, and possibility.

So first and foremost, I want to thank Baron Baptiste, the creator of Baptiste yoga. I also thank my yoga community at Hot Spot Power Yoga for pushing me and sustaining me on my heart journey.

And yes, it's true – no writer does her work alone. I thank my dear friend and editor Julie Carpenter. I am deeply grateful to you for your love and support. You are an amazing writer. (Readers, you must check out her work! www.sacredchickens.com.)

Introduction

Mindfulness is the practice of living in the moment with focused attention. Learning to set aside our random, unhelpful thoughts to focus our attention to our present experience is a life-changing practice. Before I found mindfulness, I often spent my days in my head, worrying, thinking, ruminating. I wanted to fully engage with life, and sometimes I would, but it was hard to sustain. My thoughts were just too powerful.

Mindfulness is like physical training for the mind. Each time we purposefully set aside our thoughts and focus on the present moment, we literally rewire our brains to think differently. Just like working a physical muscle, it takes repetition and practice. It's really a lifestyle change.

> *When we spend so much time in our heads, we take ourselves out of the only time we really have, which is now. Our runaway minds rob us of our very lives.*

This is not an easy practice. Our modern world is highly stimulating and can easily distract us from our path. That's what led me to focus on my heart. When we add heart into our mindfulness practice, we fill up ourselves with our heartfelt intention which creates a fertile garden of mind and soul. We free up the path to become our best selves.

Treat this journal as an accountability partner, reminding you to take time to grow your mindfulness practice. Know that this practice is for you. If you miss a day or feel you aren't giving it your all, be kind to yourself. Don't berate or shame yourself. Make this practice your own, one that fits where you are now.

The meditation exercises can be particularly challenging, especially if you're new. Again, make the meditation your own. You may feel that you have to be a yogi to get it right. Know that THERE IS NO RIGHT. There is no goal to achieve. The work is in just carving out the time to be quiet. You absolutely do not have to do it any particular way. Take the physical position that's comfortable for you. You can sit, lie down, lean against the wall. Try out eyes closed or open with a soft gaze. It's okay if you don't meditate every day – the practice is beneficial no matter if you do it daily, once a week or once a month.

When you feel like quitting, remember you are working a new muscle in your brain, and just like physical exercise, mind training takes time. I encourage you to hang in there and see what happens. Expect to spend 15-20 minutes a day.

Mindfulness exercises are designed to shift your focus to something happening right now, providing a short-circuit to negative thinking. Don't be fooled by their simplicity though. They really work!

- ❧ **Mindfulness makes us feel more alive.** Thoughts are a way to check out, to numb our experiences.
- ❧ **Mindfulness improves our ability to listen.** Imagine how happy your loved ones will be!
- ❧ **Mindfulness makes our relationships richer.** Better listening and focusing improves our connection.
- ❧ **Mindfulness improves focus.** Better focus helps in every area of life (job, relationships, hobbies... even driving).
- ❧ **Mindfulness grows gratitude.** As we sharpen our skills to truly see, our appreciation grows for the people and abundance we have.

I used to think negative thoughts were unhealthy and needed to be stopped. I now understand that negative thoughts can't be stopped. But what we can do is practice shifting our focus and letting our thoughts fade into the background. Regular mindfulness practice turns down their volume so they stop stealing the show.

My sincere hope is this journal will help you on your path to living more heartfully. It's time to get out of your head and into your heart!

Day 1: _____

Reframe One Negative Thought You Had Today

Reframing negative thoughts trains your brain to consider more positive, heart-filled alternatives. Because negative thoughts take us out of the present moment and into our heads, practicing reframing helps us to move past thoughts quickly so we can return to what's in our hearts.

Give it a try! Reword a negative thought into a positive, compassionate, heart-filled thought.

Negative Thought	Positive/Heart-filled Alternative
Example:	Example:
I never do anything right.	*I sometimes make mistakes; no one is perfect.*

_____ _____

_____ _____

_____ _____

_____ _____

_____ _____

_____ _____

_____ _____

_____ _____

_____ _____

_____ _____

> Make space in your heart for yourself. Don't expect to do anything in this journal "right." If you can't fill in all the blanks, who cares? Focus on what you can do, your possibilities. Let go of perfection. Be gentle with yourself. Go slow.

Gratitude List

It's natural for our brains to be overrun with judgment, negativity, worries. Gratitude is an expression of the heart. Taking this time to think with our hearts has similar effects as reframing. We train our brains to focus away from the negative toward light and ease. We rediscover those things we often overlook and take for granted. Focusing on the little things is where the magic of mindfulness lives.

> Don't know where to start? Here are some things to be grateful for: clean running water, roof over your head, air conditioning, clean air to breathe.

Try it! List 5 things you are grateful for.

- ✍ _____
- ✍ _____
- ✍ _____
- ✍ _____
- ✍ _____

Successes

We can be so hard on ourselves. We treat ourselves in a way we would never treat our friends. Can you open your heart to your best friend, you? Start by seeing and stop overlooking your accomplishments. Take note of the things you do each day, big and small. See it not as bragging, but as making kindness your daily practice.

Give it a try! List 3 things you did well today.

- ✍ _____
- ✍ _____
- ✍ _____

> Don't discount the power of small successes. Sometimes just getting out of bed is an achievement! Celebrate your little successes too!

Day 2: _____

Reframe One Negative Thought You Had Today
Reword a negative thought into a positive, heart-filled one.

Negative Thought
Example:
She thinks I'm incompetent.

Positive/Rational Alternative
Example:
I am a hard-working person striving to learn from my mistakes.

_____   _____
_____   _____
_____   _____
_____   _____
_____   _____
_____   _____

Gratitude List
List 5 things you are grateful for.

More ideas: heart pumping blood, pets/people you love, things you enjoy

- _____
- _____
- _____
- _____
- _____

Successes
Pat yourself on the back for 3 things you did well today.

Being able to focus and really enjoy a meal is a success. Taking care of your teeth protects your heart's health.

- _____
- _____
- _____

Reframe One Negative Thought You Had Today

Reword a negative thought into a positive or rational one.

Negative Thought	**Positive/Rational Alternative**
Example:	Example:
I can't stop feeling scared.	*I am a courageous person working on facing my fears.*

_____   _____
_____   _____
_____   _____
_____   _____
_____   _____
_____   _____

Gratitude List

List 5 things you are grateful for.

> Name a person you love, or someone who inspired you or touched your heart.

- ✌ _____
- ✌ _____
- ✌ _____
- ✌ _____
- ✌ _____

Successes

Pat yourself on the back for 3 things you did well today.

> Being in the moment and feeling hope and joy is a success. Record such times.

- ✌ _____
- ✌ _____
- ✌ _____

Day 4: _____

Reframe One Negative Thought You Had Today

Reword a negative thought into a positive or rational one.

Negative Thought	**Positive/Rational Alternative**
Example:	Example:
I'll never get better.	*I make progress every day. I am allowing my illness to teach me more about myself.*

_____ _____

_____ _____

_____ _____

_____ _____

_____ _____

_____ _____

Gratitude List

List 5 things you are grateful for.

> The people and animals in your life are gifts.

❧ _____

❧ _____

❧ _____

❧ _____

❧ _____

Successes

Pat yourself on the back for 3 things you did well today.

❧ _____

❧ _____

❧ _____

> Mundane things like cooking and cleaning are successes too, particularly when you are ill, sad, or tired.

Great Job!

Now that you've practiced the foundation of the journal,
we'll add a mindfulness exercise every few days.
Below is the first one.

Approach these mindfulness exercises with as much ease as
possible. Do not struggle with them. There is no perfect way
to do them. Let yourself be messy.

Enjoy the journey.

First Mindfulness Assignment:
Heart Pulse

Once a day, feel your pulse. Place your peace
fingers on the inside of your wrist or on your neck
near your Adam's apple. Think about why you
have a pulse. Your heart pumps blood with
powerful force through your arteries into your
body, then through the veins to your lungs and
back to your heart. Round and round it goes. Each
pulse is a beat of your heart. Be in wonderment of
your heart. Be grateful for this life force.

Day 5: _____

Reframe One Negative Thought You Had Today
Reword a negative thought into a positive or rational one.

Negative Thought   **Positive/Rational Alternative**

_____   _____

_____   _____

_____   _____

_____   _____

_____   _____

_____   _____

Gratitude List
List 5 things you are grateful for.

> Having a home to live in, bed to sleep in, kitchen to cook in – all things to be grateful for.

- _____
- _____
- _____
- _____
- _____

Successes
Pat yourself on the back for 3 things you did well today.

- _____
- _____
- _____

> Thinking even one kind thought a day is a success when we're depressed or angry.

Mindfulness Assignment: Heart Pulse

Write about your experience with the mindfulness exercise. What did you notice? How did it feel to focus on the physicality of your heart? Were you able to keep your focus on your pulse? What thoughts did you have? If you didn't do the assignment, what got in the way?

_____

_____

_____

_____

_____

_____

_____

_____

_____

_____

_____

_____

_____

> "Mindfulness is the aware, balanced acceptance of the present experience. It isn't more complicated than that. It is opening to or receiving the present moment, pleasant or unpleasant, just as it is, without either clinging to it or rejecting it."
>
> -Sylvia Boorstein

_____

_____

_____

_____

_____

_____

_____

_____

_____

_____

_____

_____

_____

_____

_____

Day 6: _____

Reframing Negative Thoughts

Now that you've done this activity for a few days, you know how to reframe negative thoughts. Try doing this on the fly as negative thoughts occur throughout the day. We won't journal this going forward. Periodically I will remind you to incorporate this as a daily habit.

Gratitude List

List 5 things you are grateful for.

- _____
- _____
- _____
- _____
- _____

Successes

Pat yourself on the back for 3 things you did well today.

- _____
- _____
- _____

Mindfulness Assignment: Heart Pulse

Write about your experiences.

_____
_____
_____
_____
_____
_____
_____
_____
_____
_____
_____
_____

Day 7: _____

Gratitude List
List 5 things you are grateful for.

-   _____
-   _____
-   _____
-   _____
-   _____

Successes
List 3 things you did well today.

-   _____
-   _____
-   _____

Mindfulness Assignment: Heart Pulse
How did the mindfulness assignment go? What did you notice?

_____

_____

_____

_____

_____

_____

_____

_____

_____

_____

_____

_____

_____

_____

_____

> *"Heartfulness is more than being in the moment, it is being in the moment with awareness of our heart. We can learn to see, hear, touch, feel the world about us through and with our heart. There is heart intelligence...being in the moment with acceptance, compassion, understanding, gratitude and qualities of our heart."*
>
> *-Bruce Davis, PhD., Huffington Post*

Day 8: _____

Gratitude List
List 5 things you are grateful for.

- _____
- _____
- _____
- _____
- _____

Successes
List 3 things you did well today.

- _____
- _____
- _____

Mindfulness Assignment: Heart Pulse
How did the mindfulness assignment go? What did you notice?

_____

_____

_____

_____

_____

_____

Next Mindfulness Assignment:
Silent Meal

Make one meal a day a silent meal. Turn off the TV, computer, any distractions. Really focus on the food as you eat. Notice aromas, texture, colors, taste. Notice how you chew and swallow. Do you put food in your mouth before you've swallowed the previous bite? Practice laying down your fork after each bite and picking it up after you've swallowed. Do you chew faster or slower when you do that? Food is nourishment for our bodies and souls. Open your heart to a new relationship with food.

Day 9: _____

Gratitude List
List 5 things you are grateful for.

- ✍ _____
- ✍ _____
- ✍ _____
- ✍ _____
- ✍ _____

Successes
List 3 things you did well today.

- ✍ _____
- ✍ _____
- ✍ _____

Mindfulness Assignment: Silent Meal
How did the mindfulness assignment go? What did you experience?
If you forgot, what got in the way? Are you beating yourself up
now for forgetting? (Don't!)

_____

_____

_____

_____

_____

_____

_____

_____

_____

_____

_____

_____

_____

_____

Day 10: _____

Gratitude List

List 5 things you are grateful for.

- _____
- _____
- _____
- _____
- _____

Successes

List 3 things you did well today.

- _____
- _____
- _____

Mindfulness Assignment: Silent Meal

Write about your experiences.

_____

_____

_____

_____

_____

_____

_____

_____

_____

"I don't have to chase extraordinary moments to find happiness - it's right in front of me if I'm paying attention and practicing gratitude."

-Brene Brown

_____

_____

_____

Day 11: _____

Gratitude List
List 5 things you are grateful for.

- ❧ _____
- ❧ _____
- ❧ _____
- ❧ _____
- ❧ _____

Successes
List 3 things you did well today.

- ❧ _____
- ❧ _____
- ❧ _____

Mindfulness Assignment: Silent Meal
Write about your experiences.

_____
_____
_____
_____
_____

Next Mindfulness Assignment:
Heart "Fix"

Every day in conversations, be on the lookout for when you try to "fix" someone or a situation. Are you listening non-judgmentally or are you passing judgment? Are you drawing conclusions or making assumptions that could be inaccurate or incomplete? Is your "fix" helpful or is it serving some need you have, like needing to be right, smart, or righteous? Does it make you feel relieved when someone has it worse than you? For the next few days, be mindful of your motives in your daily interactions with people. What do you really, truly want? True connection starts with heart. Look for opportunities to engage your heart.

Day 12: _____

Gratitude List
List 5 things you are grateful for.

- ✐ _____
- ✐ _____
- ✐ _____
- ✐ _____
- ✐ _____

Successes
List 3 things you did well today.

- ✐ _____
- ✐ _____
- ✐ _____

Mindfulness Assignment: Heart "Fix"
How did the assignment go? What did you experience? Did checking your motives change your perspective? How did it feel to connect with heart?

_____

_____

_____

_____

_____

_____

_____

_____

_____

_____

_____

_____

_____

_____

_____

_____

Day 13:

Gratitude List
List 5 things you are grateful for.

- _____
- _____
- _____
- _____
- _____

Successes
List 3 things you did well today.

- _____
- _____
- _____

Mindfulness Assignment: Heart "Fix"
Write about your experiences.

_____
_____
_____
_____
_____
_____
_____
_____
_____
_____
_____
_____
_____
_____
_____
_____
_____
_____

Day 14: _____

Gratitude List
List 5 things you are grateful for.

- _____
- _____
- _____
- _____
- _____

Successes
List 3 things you did well today.

- _____
- _____
- _____

Mindfulness Assignment: Heart "Fix"
Write about your experiences.

_____

_____

_____

_____

_____

_____

_____

_____

_____

_____

_____

_____

_____

> As you complete your gratitude and successes each day, try not to be repetitive. It's easy to fall into a rut of repeating the same things over and over in your journal. Challenge yourself to think differently. Even if it's the same thought, reword it so it has a slightly different meaning. See the appendix for ways I've done this.

Day 15:

Gratitude List
List 5 things you are grateful for.

- ✟ _____
- ✟ _____
- ✟ _____
- ✟ _____
- ✟ _____

Successes
List 3 things you did well today.

- ✟ _____
- ✟ _____
- ✟ _____

Mindfulness Assignment: Heart "Fix"
Write about your experiences.

_____

_____

_____

_____

_____

_____

_____

_____

"We don't stop playing because we grow old. We grow old because we stop playing."

–George Bernard Shaw

_____

_____

_____

_____

_____

_____

_____

_____

Day 16: _____

Gratitude List
List 5 things you are grateful for.

- _____
- _____
- _____
- _____
- _____

Successes
List 3 things you did well today.

- _____
- _____
- _____

Mindfulness Assignment: Heart "Fix"
Write about your experiences.

_____
_____
_____
_____
_____

Mega Mindfulness Assignment:
Thought Watching Meditation
Every day, take a 5-minute mindfulness break to meditate. Find a quiet spot with no interruptions. Sit or lie down, eyes open or closed. Don't worry about doing it right. Breathe normally. As thoughts come up, watch them pass by like on a TV screen. Notice how thoughts have a beginning and an end. Focus on the split second in between thoughts - the soundless, empty space of no thoughts. Keep watching this place of rest in between. Know that your thoughts are not the only things in your mind, there's also this mysterious stillness in you. Be with the stillness and open to your truth.

Day 17:

Gratitude List

List 5 things you are grateful for.

- _____
- _____
- _____
- _____
- _____

Successes

List 3 things you did well today.

- _____
- _____
- _____

Mindfulness Assignment: Thought Watching Meditation

How did meditation go? Were you able to see thoughts without judgement float by? Were you able to focus on the space in between? What did you notice when you connected with your stillness?

_____

_____

_____

_____

_____

_____

_____

_____

_____

_____

_____

_____

_____

_____

Day 18: _____

Gratitude List
List 5 things you are grateful for.

- ➥ _____
- ➥ _____
- ➥ _____
- ➥ _____
- ➥ _____

Successes
List 3 things you did well today.

- ➥ _____
- ➥ _____
- ➥ _____

Mindfulness Assignment: Thought Watching Meditation
Write about your experiences.

_____
_____
_____
_____
_____
_____
_____
_____
_____
_____
_____
_____
_____
_____
_____
_____
_____
_____

Day 19: _____

Gratitude List
List 5 things you are grateful for.

- _____
- _____
- _____
- _____
- _____

Successes
List 3 things you did well today.

- _____
- _____
- _____

Mindfulness Assignment: Thought Watching Meditation
Write about your experiences.

_____

_____

_____

_____

_____   *"There are selfish benefits to not being an a**hole...numerous studies show that compassionate people are happier, healthier, more popular and more successful."*

_____   *-Dan Harris, NBC anchor, author of "10% Happier"*

_____

_____

_____

_____

_____

_____

_____

Day 20: _____

Gratitude List
List 5 things you are grateful for.

- ❧ _____
- ❧ _____
- ❧ _____
- ❧ _____
- ❧ _____

> Name a person.
> Write down one
> thing you like
> about them.
> Repeat daily until
> you run out of
> ideas. You may
> find you appreciate
> far more about
> them than you
> realize.

Successes
List 3 things you did well today.

- ❧ _____
- ❧ _____
- ❧ _____

Mindfulness Assignment: Thought Watching Meditation
Write about your experiences.

_____
_____
_____
_____
_____

_____
_____
_____
_____
_____
_____
_____

"Meditation has suffered from poor PR because most people think that meditation is for fans of aromatherapy, Enya, and Ultimate Frisbee. After all it was brought to this country by beat poets, hippies, and rogue gurus. But what's changed is the science. Studies are strongly suggestive of a long list of very attractive benefits, lower blood pressure, boosting the immune system, reducing the release of the stress hormone cortisol. Neuroscience suggests it rewires the brain for happiness. I think meditation will be the next public health revolution."

-Dan Harris, NBC anchor, author of "10% Happier"

Day 21: _____

Gratitude List
List 5 things you are grateful for.

- ⁎ _____
- ⁎ _____
- ⁎ _____
- ⁎ _____
- ⁎ _____

Successes
List 3 things you did well today.

- ⁎ _____
- ⁎ _____
- ⁎ _____

Mindfulness Assignment: Thought Watching Meditation
Write about your experiences.

_____

_____

_____

_____

_____

Next Mindfulness Assignment:
Water Gratitude

A former boss of mine who served in the Middle East once told me the thing he missed most was clean water. He described how he didn't always have running water and had to walk to a water source be it a community pump or a local river. He would have to purify the water before using it. It took hours each day just to get clean water. Clean water arriving through pipes to our homes and businesses is wondrous. Imagine what it would be like without it. This week, whenever you interact with water (dishwashing, bathing, laundry, handwashing) think of how grateful you are.

(Thank you, Mark Ghirardi, you me influenced me more than you know.)

Day 22: _____

Gratitude List
List 5 things you are grateful for.

- _____
- _____
- _____
- _____
- _____

Successes
List 3 things you did well today.

- _____
- _____
- _____

Mindfulness Assignment: Water Gratitude
How did your mindfulness assignment go? Did your appreciation of water change? Did your physical experience with water change? What was it like doing mundane things with intention and gratitude?

_____
_____
_____
_____
_____
_____
_____
_____
_____
_____
_____
_____
_____
_____

Day 23: _____

Gratitude List
List 5 things you are grateful for.

- ✍ _____
- ✍ _____
- ✍ _____
- ✍ _____
- ✍ _____

Successes
List 3 things you did well today.

- ✍ _____
- ✍ _____
- ✍ _____

Mindfulness Assignment: Water Gratitude
Write about your experiences.

_____
_____
_____
_____
_____
_____
_____
_____
_____
_____
_____
_____
_____
_____
_____
_____

"Teacher: How can we get some clean water?"
"Student: bring the water from the river and wash it."
- Anas Skizo

Day 24: _____

Gratitude List
List 5 things you are grateful for.

- _____
- _____
- _____
- _____
- _____

Successes
List 3 things you did well today.

- _____
- _____
- _____

Mindfulness Assignment: Water Gratitude
Write about your experiences.

_____
_____
_____
_____
_____
_____
_____
_____
_____
_____
_____
_____
_____
_____
_____
_____
_____
_____

Day 25:

Gratitude List

List 5 things you are grateful for.

- _____
- _____
- _____
- _____
- _____

Successes

List 3 things you did well today.

- _____
- _____
- _____

Mindfulness Assignment: Water Gratitude

Write about your experiences.

_____
_____
_____
_____
_____
_____
_____
_____
_____
_____
_____
_____
_____
_____
_____
_____
_____

Mega Mindfulness Assignment:
Heart-Based Living

Do you find yourself unfulfilled and wishing for more? Do you feel you're not living to your full potential? Wonder what your purpose is? Whether you know your path and need help staying true to it, or don't know your path at all, values-based living can clear the way. By living our values, we consciously choose to stand up for what's in our heart. We see opportunities we've overlooked before and gain more confidence to live authentically.

Step 1:
Write down 3 or 4 values (e.g., compassion, generosity, authenticity). Choose values that ring in your heart.

Step 2:
Throughout each day, be mindful of your actions and reactions. Do they reflect your values? Are you doing things that undermine them? Write down how you can serve your values better. As you shift your thinking and behaviors to align with your values, your heart will reveal itself. You'll better see the connection between what's in your heart and what you express in the world, empowering you to make meaningful changes.

Tip:
The appendix has a list of values and additional guidance for this mega assignment.

Day 26: _____

Gratitude List
List 5 things you are grateful for.

 _____
 _____
 _____
 _____
 _____

Successes
List 3 things you did well today.

 _____
 _____
 _____

Mega Mindfulness Assignment: Heart-Based Living
Write down your 3-4 values and examples of how you lived them in the last 24 hours. Did you do anything that undermined them? What are some ideas for better serving your heart next time?

_____

_____

_____

_____

_____

_____

_____

_____

_____

_____

_____

_____

_____

_____

_____

_____

_____

Day 27: ____________

Gratitude List

List 5 things you are grateful for.

- ____________
- ____________
- ____________
- ____________
- ____________

Catch the moment!
This week, give full attention to your colleagues. Move away from your email, stop texting, and really listen to them. When they approach you and you're busy, stop what you're doing and be present with them.

Successes

List 3 things you did well today.

- ____________
- ____________
- ____________

Mega Mindfulness Assignment: Heart-Based Living

Write about your experiences.

<u>Day 28:</u>

Gratitude List
List 5 things you are grateful for.

- ❧ _____
- ❧ _____
- ❧ _____
- ❧ _____
- ❧ _____

Successes
List 3 things you did well today.

- ❧ _____
- ❧ _____
- ❧ _____

Mega Mindfulness Assignment: Heart-Based Living
Write about your experiences.

_____

_____

_____

_____

_____

_____

_____

_____

_____

_____

_____

> *"A lot of people think if they get happy they will lose their edge. That is not the proposition of mindfulness. Mindfulness is about helping you focus and not get jerked around by your emotions, and compassion is about not getting blinded by anger, hatred and ill will so you make stupid decisions."*
>
> *– Dan Harris, NBC anchor, author of "10% Happier"*

_____

_____

_____

_____

_____

_____

_____

Day 29: _____

Gratitude List
List 5 things you are grateful for.

- _____
- _____
- _____
- _____
- _____

Successes
List 3 things you did well today.

- _____
- _____
- _____

Mega Mindfulness Assignment: Heart-Based Living
Write about your experiences.

_____

_____

_____

_____

_____

_____

_____

_____

_____

_____

_____

_____

_____

_____

_____

Day 30: _____

Gratitude List
List 5 things you are grateful for.

- _____
- _____
- _____
- _____
- _____

Successes
List 3 things you did well today.

This is day 30! You've done this journal for 30 days! Celebrate that success!

- _____
- _____
- _____

Mega Mindfulness Assignment: Heart-Based Living
Write about your experiences.

_____
_____
_____
_____
_____
_____
_____

Next Mindfulness Assignment:
Silent Listening
For five minutes every day, sit alone in a place of your choosing with eyes closed. Focus on the sounds around you. Tune in. What all do you hear? What's nearby and what's off in the distance? Don't analyze or try to understand the sounds. Listen without judgment. If thoughts intrude, breathe in and out to blow them away, and return to listening.

Day 31: _____

Gratitude List
List 5 things you are grateful for.

- _____
- _____
- _____
- _____
- _____

Successes
List 3 things you did well today.

- _____
- _____
- _____

Mindfulness Assignment: Silent Listening
How was silent listening? What did you see hear off in the distance?
What sounds were close by? Did you notice your mind wandering?
Were you able to set aside thoughts and listen? What was it like to
be more mindful?

_____
_____
_____
_____
_____
_____
_____
_____
_____
_____
_____
_____
_____
_____
_____
_____

Day 32:

Gratitude List
List 5 things you are grateful for.

- _____
- _____
- _____
- _____
- _____

Successes
List 3 things you did well today.

- _____
- _____
- _____

Mindfulness Assignment: Silent Listening
Write about your experiences.

_____
_____
_____
_____
_____
_____
_____
_____
_____
_____
_____
_____
_____
_____
_____
_____
_____
_____

Day 33: _____

Gratitude List
List 5 things you are grateful for.

- _____
- _____
- _____
- _____
- _____

Successes
List 3 things you did well today.

- _____
- _____
- _____

Mindfulness Assignment: Silent Listening
Write about your experiences.

_____
_____
_____
_____
_____
_____
_____
_____
_____
_____
_____
_____
_____
_____
_____
_____
_____
_____

"Give yourself a gift of five minutes of contemplation in awe of everything you see around you. Go outside and turn your attention to the many miracles around you. This five-minute-a-day regimen of appreciation and gratitude will help you to focus your life in awe."

-Wayne Dyer

Day 34: _____

Gratitude List
List 5 things you are grateful for.

- 🕮 _____
- 🕮 _____
- 🕮 _____
- 🕮 _____
- 🕮 _____

Successes
List 3 things you did well today.

- 🕮 _____
- 🕮 _____
- 🕮 _____

Mindfulness Assignment: Silent Listening
Write about your experiences.

_____

_____

_____

_____

_____

Next Mindfulness Assignment:
Open Heart
At least once a day clasp your hands behind your back. Squeeze your shoulder blades together as your chest expands. Lift your chin to allow your chest to expand even further and breathe deep in and out through your nose. With each breath, feel your heart open up. Visualize that you are allowing your heart to lead your way. You are opening yourself to new experiences and bigger relationships. What's possible if you lead with your heart?
~ extra assignment ~
When someone or something annoys you, take a breath and look for what you can be grateful for in the situation.

Day 35: _____

Gratitude List
List 5 things you are grateful for.

- _____
- _____
- _____
- _____
- _____

Successes
List 3 things you did well today.

- _____
- _____
- _____

Mindfulness Assignment: Open Heart

How did the assignment go? What sensations did you notice in your body? How did physically opening your heart change your perception? Did you do the extra assignment to feel gratitude for an annoying person? What opportunities opened up for you?

_____
_____
_____
_____
_____
_____
_____
_____
_____
_____
_____
_____
_____
_____
_____

Day 36: _____

Gratitude List
List 5 things you are grateful for.

-   _____
-   _____
-   _____
-   _____
-   _____

Successes
List 3 things you did well today.

-   _____
-   _____
-   _____

Mindfulness Assignment: Open Heart
Write about your experiences.

_____

_____

_____

_____

_____

_____

_____

_____

_____

_____

_____

_____

_____

_____

_____

_____

_____

_____

Day 37: _____

Gratitude List
List 5 things you are grateful for.

- _____
- _____
- _____
- _____
- _____

Successes
List 3 things you did well today.

- _____
- _____
- _____

Mindfulness Assignment: Open Heart
Write about your experiences.

_____

_____

_____

_____

_____

_____

_____

_____

_____

_____

_____

_____

_____

_____

Make a moment!
Studies show that hobbies utilizing repetitive movements like knitting, coloring, Zen tangling, car repair, and painting, have similar benefits as meditation when done regularly. Perhaps it's time for a new hobby!

Gratitude List

List 5 things you are grateful for.

- _____
- _____
- _____
- _____
- _____

Successes

List 3 things you did well today.

- _____
- _____
- _____

Mindfulness Assignment: Open Heart

Write about your experiences.

_____

_____

_____

_____

_____

Next Mindfulness Assignment:
Mindful Listening Walk

Every day, go for a 5-10 minute mindful walk outdoors.
No music. No cell phone. Just you and your
environment. Tune in to your hearing. Maybe there's
an airplane in the distance, birds chirping, leaves or
snow crunching beneath your feet. What other sounds
do you hear? Don't analyze or wonder about the
sounds; experience them with a child's heart. If you find
yourself getting deep in thought, imagine placing the
thoughts on a cloud and letting them float away and
return your focus to the sounds.

Day 39: _____

Gratitude List
List 5 things you are grateful for.

- _____
- _____
- _____
- _____
- _____

Successes
List 3 things you did well today.

- _____
- _____
- _____

Mindfulness Assignment: Mindful Listening Walk
What was it like to focus on sounds on your walk? Did you hear sounds you hadn't noticed before? Were you able to stay focused on the sounds or did your mind wander? What was that like?

_____

_____

_____

_____

_____

_____

_____

_____

_____

_____

_____

_____

_____

_____

Gratitude List

List 5 things you are grateful for.

- ✍ _____
- ✍ _____
- ✍ _____
- ✍ _____
- ✍ _____

Successes

List 3 things you did well today.

- ✍ _____
- ✍ _____
- ✍ _____

Mindfulness Assignment: Mindful Listening Walk

Write about your experiences.

_____

_____

_____

_____

_____

_____

_____

_____

_____

_____

_____

_____

_____

_____

_____

_____

_____

_____

Day 41: _____

Gratitude List
List 5 things you are grateful for.

- _____
- _____
- _____
- _____
- _____

Successes
List 3 things you did well today.

- _____
- _____
- _____

Mindfulness Assignment: Mindful Listening Walk
Write about your experiences.

_____
_____
_____
_____
_____
_____
_____
_____
_____
_____
_____
_____
_____
_____
_____
_____
_____
_____

Day 42: _____

Gratitude List
List 5 things you are grateful for.

- _____
- _____
- _____
- _____
- _____

Successes
List 3 things you did well today.

- _____
- _____
- _____

Mindfulness Assignment: Mindful Listening Walk
Write about your experiences.

_____

_____

_____

_____

_____

_____

_____

_____

_____

Next Mindfulness Assignment:
Generous Listening Part 1
As people speak this week, resist the urge to interrupt
and let them speak. Resist the urge to rehearse what
you're going to say next and instead focus on what they
are saying. Breathe into your chest and imagine that
your heart is receiving what they are sharing.

Day 43: _____

Gratitude List
List 5 things you are grateful for.

- ℴ _____
- ℴ _____
- ℴ _____
- ℴ _____
- ℴ _____

Successes
List 3 things you did well today.

- ℴ _____
- ℴ _____
- ℴ _____

Mindfulness Assignment: Generous Listening Part 1
What was it like to listen more generously? Were you able to set aside your ego and give them your full attention? Did this help you feel present and connected? What feelings came up?

_____
_____
_____
_____
_____
_____
_____
_____
_____
_____
_____
_____
_____
_____
_____
_____
_____

Gratitude List

List 5 things you are grateful for.

- _____
- _____
- _____
- _____
- _____

Successes

List 3 things you did well today.

- _____
- _____
- _____

Mindfulness Assignment: Generous Listening Part 1

Write about your experiences.

_____

_____

_____

_____

_____

_____

_____

"People are illogical, unreasonable, and self-centered. Love them anyway."

– Kent Keith, From the book "The Pocket Therapist" by Therese Borchard

Consider this is true for yourself as well – love yourself anyway!

Day 45: _____

Gratitude List
List 5 things you are grateful for.

- ✍ _____
- ✍ _____
- ✍ _____
- ✍ _____
- ✍ _____

Successes
List 3 things you did well today.

- ✍ _____
- ✍ _____
- ✍ _____

Mindfulness Assignment: Generous Listening Part 1
Write about your experiences.

_____
_____
_____
_____
_____
_____
_____
_____
_____
_____
_____
_____
_____
_____
_____
_____

> **Reframing reminder**
> *How are you doing with mentally reframing your negative thoughts? This can help you when dealing with people. Rather than judging, imagine you know absolutely nothing about this person. Can you acknowledge them with an open heart instead?*

Day 46:

Gratitude List
List 5 things you are grateful for.

-   _____
-   _____
-   _____
-   _____
-   _____

Successes
List 3 things you did well today.

-   _____
-   _____
-   _____

Mindfulness Assignment: Generous Listening Part 1
Write about your experiences.

_____

_____

_____

_____

_____

_____

_____

_____

_____

Next Mindfulness Assignment:
Breathing Heart
Every day, take five minutes to sit in a room in complete quiet. Hold your head high, and breathe deep into your chest, fully expanding your heart with each breath. Notice the subtle sensations in your upper body. Feel the air in your lungs. Notice what your mind does when you physically open your heart.

Day 47: _____

Gratitude List
List 5 things you are grateful for.

- ✍ _____
- ✍ _____
- ✍ _____
- ✍ _____
- ✍ _____

Successes
List 3 things you did well today.

- ✍ _____
- ✍ _____
- ✍ _____

Mindfulness Assignment: Breathing Heart
What did you feel in your heart and body? What did your mind do? Was your mind quieter even if only for a moment? Can you use this experience to quiet the mind even when it's not quiet around you?

_____
_____
_____
_____
_____
_____
_____
_____
_____
_____
_____
_____
_____
_____
_____
_____
_____

Day 48: _____

Gratitude List
List 5 things you are grateful for.

℮ _____
℮ _____
℮ _____
℮ _____
℮ _____

Successes
List 3 things you did well today.

℮ _____
℮ _____
℮ _____

Mindfulness Assignment: Breathing Heart
Write about your experiences.

_____
_____
_____
_____
_____
_____
_____
_____
_____
_____
_____
_____
_____
_____
_____
_____
_____

Day 49: _____

Gratitude List
List 5 things you are grateful for.

- _____
- _____
- _____
- _____
- _____

Successes
List 3 things you did well today.

- _____
- _____
- _____

Mindfulness Assignment: Breathing Heart
Write about your experiences.

_____
_____
_____
_____
_____
_____
_____
_____
_____
_____
_____
_____
_____
_____
_____
_____
_____

Catch the moment!
Drink a hot drink and savor the experience. Feel the warmth on your face, the aroma, the heat on your hands. Breathe in the comfort.

Day 50: _____

Gratitude List
List 5 things you are grateful for.

    ✍ _____
    ✍ _____
    ✍ _____
    ✍ _____
    ✍ _____

Successes
List 3 things you did well today.

    ✍ _____
    ✍ _____
    ✍ _____

Mindfulness Assignment: Breathing Heart
Write about your experiences.

_____

_____

_____

_____

_____

_____

_____

_____

_____

_____

_____

_____

_____

_____

_____

_____

Day 51: _____

Gratitude List

List 5 things you are grateful for.

- _____
- _____
- _____
- _____
- _____

Successes

List 3 things you did well today.

- _____
- _____
- _____

Mindfulness Assignment: Breathing Heart

Write about your experiences.

_____

_____

_____

_____

_____

Next Mindfulness Assignment:
Heart Hugs

Every day, give someone a big hug. As you hug, feel your heart opening to the person. Enjoy and really feel the hug and this openness of heart. If you struggle focusing on heart, breathe in to physically expand your heart space. Later in the day, ponder on the experience of opening your heart to someone.

~ extra assignment ~

As people speak this week, resist the urge to speak a lot. Consider there may be no need to offer up a fix or even tell your own story. Consider what it means to listen with your heart and give people the space to tell their stories without being "one-upped" by your stories.

Day 52:

Gratitude List
List 5 things you are grateful for.

- _____
- _____
- _____
- _____
- _____

Successes
List 3 things you did well today.

- _____
- _____
- _____

Mindfulness Assignment: Heart Hugs
Did you heartfully hug someone today? Did anything in your heart or mind stop you from fully being in the hug? Did you do the extra assignment of quieting your tongue and really listening?

_____
_____
_____
_____
_____
_____
_____
_____
_____
_____
_____
_____
_____
_____
_____

Day 53: _____

Gratitude List
List 5 things you are grateful for.

- ✍ _____
- ✍ _____
- ✍ _____
- ✍ _____
- ✍ _____

Successes
List 3 things you did well today.

- ✍ _____
- ✍ _____
- ✍ _____

Mindfulness Assignment: Heart Hugs
Write about your experiences.

_____
_____
_____
_____
_____
_____
_____
_____
_____
_____
_____
_____
_____
_____

"The more you need people to agree with you, the less open you are to what they think, feel, and believe. You cannot share with them because you are trying to change them, and they cannot share with you because you are not listening."

-Gary Zukav

Day 54: _____

Gratitude List
List 5 things you are grateful for.

- ✍ _____
- ✍ _____
- ✍ _____
- ✍ _____
- ✍ _____

Successes
List 3 things you did well today.

- ✍ _____
- ✍ _____
- ✍ _____

Mindfulness Assignment: Heart Hugs
Write about your experiences.

_____
_____
_____
_____
_____
_____

Next Mindfulness Assignment:
Heart in Words

Every day, notice how often you use the words "we" or "you" when you really mean "I". How often do you use these words to sound inclusive when you're really expressing your own experience or opinion? Open your heart and own your stories. Practice putting your heart into your words and intention by saying "I." You may find others more readily share their stories when you don't assume others are walking your path. See the Appendix for more on this exercise.

Day 55: _____

Gratitude List
List 5 things you are grateful for.

- ❧ _____
- ❧ _____
- ❧ _____
- ❧ _____
- ❧ _____

Successes
List 3 things you did well today.

- ❧ _____
- ❧ _____
- ❧ _____

Mindfulness Assignment: Heart in Words
How did it feel to own your stories? Did you experience a shift in perception?

_____
_____
_____
_____
_____
_____
_____
_____
_____
_____
_____
_____
_____
_____
_____
_____
_____

Day 56: _____

Gratitude List
List 5 things you are grateful for.

- _____
- _____
- _____
- _____
- _____

Successes
List 3 things you did well today.

- _____
- _____
- _____

Mindfulness Assignment: Heart in Words
Write about your experiences.

_____

_____

_____

_____

_____

_____

_____

_____

_____

_____

_____

> *"The language we use influences the way we think."*
>
> *- Steven Pinker*

_____

_____

_____

Day 57: _____

Gratitude List
List 5 things you are grateful for.

- _____
- _____
- _____
- _____
- _____

Successes
List 3 things you did well today.

- _____
- _____
- _____

Mindfulness Assignment: Heart in Words
Write about your experiences.

_____

_____

_____

_____

_____

_____

_____

Next Mindfulness Assignment:
Nature in Detail

Go outside to sit or walk. Use your five senses to experience the outdoors. Focus on each sense, one by one, giving yourself at least a full minute to experience each one. See around you, smell the aromas, listen to the sounds, feel and taste the air. If distracting thoughts occur, let them float off into the background of your mind, then return your focus to the sense you're experiencing. Let your senses come

Day 58:

Gratitude List

List 5 things you are grateful for.

- ‿ _____
- ‿ _____
- ‿ _____
- ‿ _____
- ‿ _____

Successes

List 3 things you did well today.

- ‿ _____
- ‿ _____
- ‿ _____

Mindfulness Assignment: Nature in Detail

How did it go? What details did you notice? Did random thoughts come? Were you able to let them float off or did they steal the show? (It's perfectly natural for thoughts to steal the show. Our practice is to notice when this happens and refocus our attention.)

_____

_____

_____

_____

_____

_____

_____

_____

_____

_____

_____

_____

_____

_____

Day 59: _____

Gratitude List
List 5 things you are grateful for.

- ❧ _____
- ❧ _____
- ❧ _____
- ❧ _____
- ❧ _____

Successes
List 3 things you did well today.

- ❧ _____
- ❧ _____
- ❧ _____

Mindfulness Assignment: Nature in Detail
Write about your experiences.

_____
_____
_____
_____
_____
_____
_____
_____
_____
_____
_____
_____
_____
_____
_____
_____
_____

Day 60: _____

Gratitude List
List 5 things you are grateful for.

- ✒ _____
- ✒ _____
- ✒ _____
- ✒ _____
- ✒ _____

Successes
List 3 things you did well today.

> **Check it out! This is day 60!** Write this success down! Whoop whoop!

- ✒ _____
- ✒ _____
- ✒ _____

Mindfulness Assignment: Nature in Detail
Write about your experiences.

_____

_____

_____

_____

_____

_____

_____

_____

_____

_____

_____

_____

_____

Reframing reminder
It's hard to change our thinking, but worth the effort. Just be careful to not get down on yourself. Negative thinking is normal! Think of reframing as an alternative, not a replacement, to negative thoughts. Don't try and force negative thoughts to disappear, instead let them take the back seat.

Day 61: _____

Gratitude List
List 5 things you are grateful for.

- _____
- _____
- _____
- _____
- _____

Successes
List 3 things you did well today.

- _____
- _____
- _____

Mindfulness Assignment: Nature in Detail
Write about your experiences.

_____
_____
_____
_____
_____

Mega Mindfulness Assignment:
Walking Meditation

Every day, take a mindful walk with no music or cell phone. Find a place where you can walk without your shoes on. Walk in a simple pattern such as walking in a figure eight or following the edge of a room. If comfortable, walk with your hands clasped behind your back, gaze forward. Breathe normally. As you walk, focus on feeling with your toes and the soles of your feet. Stay focused on physical sensation. (If walking is not accessible, an alternative is to move the body in a repeating pattern while in a quiet place to focus on sensations.)

Day 62: _____

Gratitude List
List 5 things you are grateful for.

- ❧ _____
- ❧ _____
- ❧ _____
- ❧ _____
- ❧ _____

Successes
List 3 things you did well today.

- ❧ _____
- ❧ _____
- ❧ _____

Mega Mindfulness Assignment: Walking Meditation
How did it go? What was it like getting quiet and moving repetitively? What thoughts came up? Were you able to let them go and stay focused on body? What feelings came up?

_____

_____

_____

_____

_____

_____

_____

_____

_____

If you find yourself getting carried away by thoughts during meditation, see if these techniques help:
-Visualize placing the thought on a leaf in a creek and watch it float away.
-Imagine physically turning your back to the thoughts.
-Name the thought "thinking" or "feeling" and return to your focus.

Day 63: _____

Gratitude List
List 5 things you are grateful for.

- _____
- _____
- _____
- _____
- _____

Successes
List 3 things you did well today.

- _____
- _____
- _____

Mega Mindfulness Assignment: Walking Meditation
Write about your experiences.

_____

_____

_____

_____

_____

_____

_____

_____

"Mindfulness is the ability to know what's happening in your head at any given moment without getting carried away by it."

-Dan Harris, NBC anchor, author of "10% Happier"

_____

_____

_____

_____

_____

_____

Day 64: _____

Gratitude List
List 5 things you are grateful for.

- _____
- _____
- _____
- _____
- _____

Successes
List 3 things you did well today.

- _____
- _____
- _____

Mega Mindfulness Assignment: Walking Meditation
Write about your experiences.

_____

_____

_____

_____

_____

_____

_____

_____

_____

_____

_____

_____

Catch the moment!
When anxiety comes up, notice how you're bracing for something to happen. Take a deep breath and fill up your heart space. See if you can let your heart be open to whatever happens.

_____

_____

_____

Day 65: _____

Gratitude List

List 5 things you are grateful for.

- _____
- _____
- _____
- _____
- _____

Successes

List 3 things you did well today.

- _____
- _____
- _____

Mega Mindfulness Assignment: Walking Meditation

Write about your experiences.

_____
_____
_____
_____
_____
_____
_____
_____

Next Mindfulness Assignment:
Generous Listening Part 2

At least once a day, make a point to really listen to someone (a colleague, friend, loved one). Stop what you're doing and give them your full attention. No cell phone, computer, etc. Look at them and listen to their words. Are you predicting what they're going to say? Are you rehearsing what you'll say next? Stop. Be in the moment. Experience their words as they speak them. Listen with your heart.

Day 66: _____

Gratitude List
List 5 things you are grateful for.

- _____
- _____
- _____
- _____
- _____

Successes
List 3 things you did well today.

- _____
- _____
- _____

Mindfulness Assignment: Generous Listening Part 2
What was it like to give someone your full attention? Were you able to be fully with them in that moment? What did you find difficult?

_____

_____

_____

_____

_____

_____

_____

_____

_____

_____

_____

_____

_____

_____

_____

_____

_____

Day 67: _____

Gratitude List
List 5 things you are grateful for.

- _____
- _____
- _____
- _____
- _____

Successes
List 3 things you did well today.

- _____
- _____
- _____

Mindfulness Assignment: Generous Listening Part 2
Write about your experiences.

_____
_____
_____
_____
_____
_____
_____
_____
_____
_____
_____
_____
_____
_____
_____
_____
_____
_____

Day 68: _____

Gratitude List
List 5 things you are grateful for.

- ✍ _____
- ✍ _____
- ✍ _____
- ✍ _____
- ✍ _____

Successes
List 3 things you did well today.

- ✍ _____
- ✍ _____
- ✍ _____

Mindfulness Assignment: Generous Listening Part 2
Write about your experiences.

_____

_____

_____

_____

_____

_____

_____

_____

_____

_____

> **Catch the moment!**
> Is there something you do for another person in your life, like their laundry or dishes? Does it annoy you? Shift this next time you perform your task. Think of what you love about that person. Breathe deep into your heart and be grateful they are in your life. Honor your heart for the love you're giving through the task.

Day 69: _____

Gratitude List
List 5 things you are grateful for.

- _____
- _____
- _____
- _____
- _____

Successes
List 3 things you did well today.

- _____
- _____
- _____

Mindfulness Assignment: Generous Listening Part 2
Write about your experiences.

_____
_____
_____
_____
_____
_____
_____
_____
_____
_____
_____
_____
_____
_____
_____
_____
_____
_____

Day 70: _____

Gratitude List

List 5 things you are grateful for.

- _____
- _____
- _____
- _____
- _____

Successes

List 3 things you did well today.

- _____
- _____
- _____

Mindfulness Assignment: Generous Listening Part 2

Write about your experiences.

_____
_____
_____
_____
_____
_____
_____
_____
_____
_____
_____
_____
_____
_____
_____
_____
_____

Day 71: _____

Gratitude List
List 5 things you are grateful for.

- ✍ _____
- ✍ _____
- ✍ _____
- ✍ _____
- ✍ _____

Successes
List 3 things you did well today.

- ✍ _____
- ✍ _____
- ✍ _____

Mindfulness Assignment: Generous Listening Part 2
Write about your experiences.

_____

_____

_____

_____

_____

_____

_____

_____

_____

_____

Next Mindfulness Assignment:
Mindful Bathing

As you bathe this week, focus on your sinuses. Breathe
in the steam, notice how your breathing changes.
Breathe in the aromas of soap and shampoo. Notice
how your sinuses fill with scent. When thoughts arise,
imagine they rinse off you and down the drain. Then
return your focus to the physical experience of bathing.

Gratitude List

List 5 things you are grateful for.

- _____
- _____
- _____
- _____
- _____

Successes

List 3 things you did well today.

- _____
- _____
- _____

Mindfulness Assignment: Mindful Bathing

What was the assignment like? How did the steam and aromas feel in your sinuses? Did other thoughts intrude? Were you able to wash them down the drain?

_____

_____

_____

_____

_____

_____

_____

_____

_____

_____

_____

_____

_____

_____

_____

_____

Day 73: _____

Gratitude List
List 5 things you are grateful for.

- _____
- _____
- _____
- _____
- _____

Successes
List 3 things you did well today.

- _____
- _____
- _____

Mindfulness Assignment: Mindful Bathing
Write about your experiences.

_____
_____
_____
_____
_____
_____
_____
_____
_____
_____
_____
_____
_____
_____
_____
_____
_____

Gratitude List
List 5 things you are grateful for.

- _____
- _____
- _____
- _____
- _____

Successes
List 3 things you did well today.

- _____
- _____
- _____

Mindfulness Assignment: Mindful Bathing
Write about your experiences.

_____

_____

_____

_____

_____

_____

_____

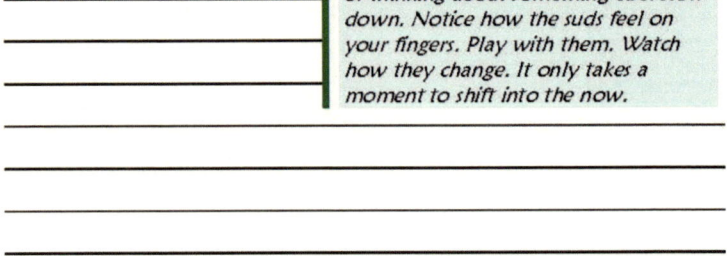

Catch the moment!
When you're washing your hands or washing dishes, notice if you're rushing or thinking about something else. Slow down. Notice how the suds feel on your fingers. Play with them. Watch how they change. It only takes a moment to shift into the now.

_____

_____

_____

_____

Day 75: _____

Gratitude List
List 5 things you are grateful for.

- _____
- _____
- _____
- _____
- _____

Successes
List 3 things you did well today.

- _____
- _____
- _____

Mindfulness Assignment: Mindful Bathing
Write about your experiences.

_____
_____
_____
_____
_____
_____
_____
_____
_____
_____
_____
_____
_____
_____
_____
_____

Reframing reminder
We can be so hard on ourselves when it comes to our bodies. Can you reframe your thoughts in this area? Instead of focusing on what your body lacks, can you focus on what it gives? Think of how your body literally carries you through your day. Place your hand on your heart and breathe in gratitude for your body.

Day 76: _____

Gratitude List
List 5 things you are grateful for.

℞ _____
℞ _____
℞ _____
℞ _____
℞ _____

Successes
List 3 things you did well today.

℞ _____
℞ _____
℞ _____

Mindfulness Assignment: Mindful Bathing
Write about your experiences.

_____
_____
_____
_____
_____
_____
_____
_____
_____
_____
_____
_____
_____
_____
_____
_____
_____
_____

Day 77: _____

Gratitude List
List 5 things you are grateful for.

- ✍ _____
- ✍ _____
- ✍ _____
- ✍ _____
- ✍ _____

Successes
List 3 things you did well today.

- ✍ _____
- ✍ _____
- ✍ _____

Mindfulness Assignment: Mindful Bathing
Write about your experiences.

_____

_____

_____

_____

_____

_____

_____

Next Mindfulness Assignment:
Un-busy Bee

Keeping busy is often a way to avoid feelings. Maybe you pace or fidget when you're bored or uncomfortable. Each day notice when you're using busyness this way. Stop, take a breath and silently acknowledge what you're doing. Don't analyze or dwell on it, just observe it. See how long you can stay in this mindful awareness.

~ extra assignment ~

At least once a day, breathe into your heart and make note of the emotions there.

Day 78: _____

Gratitude List
List 5 things you are grateful for.

_____
_____
_____
_____
_____

Successes
List 3 things you did well today.

_____
_____
_____

Mindfulness Assignments: Un-Busy Bee
Were you able to catch yourself using busyness to avoid feelings? What was it like to simply observe this? Did you do the extra assignment and breathe into the emotions in your heart? What came up for you?

_____
_____
_____
_____
_____
_____
_____
_____
_____
_____
_____
_____
_____
_____
_____

Day 79: _____

Gratitude List
List 5 things you are grateful for.

- _____
- _____
- _____
- _____
- _____

Successes
List 3 things you did well today.

- _____
- _____
- _____

Mindfulness Assignment: Un-Busy Bee
Write about your experiences.

_____
_____
_____
_____
_____
_____
_____
_____
_____

> " 'Crazy-busy' is a great armor, it's a great way for numbing. What a lot of us do is that we stay so busy, and so out in front of our life, that the truth of how we're feeling and what we really need can't catch up with us."
>
> — Brene Brown

_____
_____

Day 80:

Gratitude List
List 5 things you are grateful for.

-   _____
-   _____
-   _____
-   _____
-   _____

Successes
List 3 things you did well today.

-   _____
-   _____
-   _____

Mindfulness Assignment: Un-Busy Bee
Write about your experiences.

_____
_____
_____
_____
_____
_____
_____
_____
_____
_____
_____
_____
_____
_____
_____
_____
_____

Day 81: _____

Gratitude List
List 5 things you are grateful for.

- _____
- _____
- _____
- _____
- _____

Successes
List 3 things you did well today.

- _____
- _____
- _____

Mindfulness Assignment: Un-Busy Bee
Write about your experiences.

_____
_____
_____
_____
_____
_____
_____
_____
_____
_____
_____
_____
_____
_____
_____
_____
_____

Day 82:

Gratitude List
List 5 things you are grateful for.

- ✍ _____
- ✍ _____
- ✍ _____
- ✍ _____
- ✍ _____

Successes
List 3 things you did well today.

- ✍ _____
- ✍ _____
- ✍ _____

Mindfulness Assignment: Un-Busy Bee
Write about your experiences.

_____

_____

_____

_____

_____

_____

_____

Next Mindfulness Assignment:
Mindful Marbles

Every day, take a 5-minute mindfulness break. Place a few marbles, pebbles, or other small round objects in your hand. Close your palms together and roll them around. Focus all attention to sensation - smoothness, coolness, sound. Soften your gaze and immerse yourself in the experience. Notice how your perception changes the longer you roll them around. If your mind wanders, gently return to your hands.

Day 83: _____

Gratitude List
List 5 things you are grateful for.

- _____
- _____
- _____
- _____
- _____

Successes
List 3 things you did well today.

- _____
- _____
- _____

Mindfulness Assignment: Mindful Marbles
Were you able to stay focused on sensations? Did you find yourself being too much in your head? Could you stop and refocus? What sensations did you feel?

_____

_____

_____

_____

_____

_____

_____

_____

_____

_____

_____

_____

_____

_____

_____

_____

Day 84: _____

Gratitude List
List 5 things you are grateful for.

- _____
- _____
- _____
- _____
- _____

Successes
List 3 things you did well today.

- _____
- _____
- _____

Mindfulness Assignment: Mindful Marbles
Write about your experiences.

_____
_____
_____
_____
_____
_____
_____
_____
_____
_____
_____
_____
_____
_____
_____
_____
_____

Day 85: _____

Gratitude List
List 5 things you are grateful for.

- ✍ _____
- ✍ _____
- ✍ _____
- ✍ _____
- ✍ _____

Successes
List 3 things you did well today.

- ✍ _____
- ✍ _____
- ✍ _____

Mindfulness Assignment: Mindful Marbles
Write about your experiences.

_____
_____
_____
_____
_____
_____
_____
_____
_____
_____
_____
_____
_____
_____
_____
_____
_____

Catch the moment!
As you brush your teeth, focus on how the brush feels against your teeth and gums. Notice which teeth you are brushing as you move along your mouth. Inhale the scent of the toothpaste. Be grateful for your teeth.

Day 86:

Gratitude List

List 5 things you are grateful for.

-
-
-
-
-

Successes

List 3 things you did well today.

-
-
-

Mindfulness Assignment: Mindful Marbles

Write about your experiences.

_____

_____

_____

_____

_____

_____

_____

_____

_____

_____

_____

_____

_____

_____

_____

_____

_____

Day 87: _____

Gratitude List
List 5 things you are grateful for.

- _____
- _____
- _____
- _____
- _____

Successes
List 3 things you did well today.

- _____
- _____
- _____

Mindfulness Assignment: Mindful Marbles
Write about your experiences.

_____

_____

_____

_____

_____

Next Mindfulness Assignment:
Breathing Meditation

Every day, take a 5-minute mindfulness break. Find a comfortable seat, place your hands palms down on your knees, and gently close your eyes. Breathe normally in/out of your nose. Nostril breathing calms the nervous system, so keep your mouth closed. Sit tall and lift your chin slightly to straighten your trachea. Draw your shoulders up and back, open your chest. If thoughts intrude, clear them away with your exhales and return focus to breath.

~ extra assignment ~

Take a pause during the day to use nostril breathing.

Day 88:

Gratitude List
List 5 things you are grateful for.

- ✍ _____
- ✍ _____
- ✍ _____
- ✍ _____
- ✍ _____

Successes
List 3 things you did well today.

- ✍ _____
- ✍ _____
- ✍ _____

Mindfulness Assignment: Breathing Meditation
Were you able to focus on your breathing? Express your gratitude for your breath? Did you do the meditation too? How did that go?

_____

_____

_____

_____

_____

_____

_____

_____

_____

_____

_____

_____

_____

_____

_____

_____

Day 89: _____

Gratitude List
List 5 things you are grateful for.

- ✍ _____
- ✍ _____
- ✍ _____
- ✍ _____
- ✍ _____

Successes
List 3 things you did well today.

- ✍ _____
- ✍ _____
- ✍ _____

Mindfulness Assignment: Breathing Meditation
Write about your experiences.

_____
_____
_____
_____
_____
_____
_____
_____
_____
_____
_____
_____
_____
_____
_____
_____
_____
_____

Day 90: _____

Gratitude List
List 5 things you are grateful for.

- ᴥ _____
- ᴥ _____
- ᴥ _____
- ᴥ _____
- ᴥ _____

Successes
List 3 things you did well today.

Three months!
Excellent work!

- ᴥ _____
- ᴥ _____
- ᴥ _____

Mindfulness Assignment: Breathing Meditation
Write about your experiences.

_____

_____

_____

_____

_____

_____

_____

_____

_____

♥

"The Tantric sages tell us that our in-breath and out-breath actually mirror the divine creative gesture. With the inhalation, we draw into our own center, our own being. With the exhalation, we expand outward into the world."

— Sally Kempton, "Awakening Shakti: The Transformative Power of the Goddesses of Yoga"

Day 91: _____

Gratitude List
List 5 things you are grateful for.

- _____
- _____
- _____
- _____
- _____

Successes
List 3 things you did well today.

- _____
- _____
- _____

Mindfulness Assignment: Breathing Meditation
Write about your experiences.

_____
_____
_____
_____
_____
_____
_____
_____
_____
_____
_____
_____
_____
_____
_____
_____
_____

Day 92: _____

Gratitude List
List 5 things you are grateful for.

- _____
- _____
- _____
- _____
- _____

Successes
List 3 things you did well today.

- _____
- _____
- _____

Mindfulness Assignment: Breathing Meditation
Write about your experiences.

_____

_____

_____

_____

_____

_____

_____

Next Mindfulness Assignment:
Heart Sight
Pick a person you interact with every day and see them with new eyes. Drop what you know about them. Let go of preconceived notions and judgments and be with them as if they're a new friend. Be curious and see what new things you learn. Feel your heart open up to them. If you feel judgment coming up, breathe deep to physically open your chest and make room for them in your heart, then release the judgment on the exhale.

Day 93:

Gratitude List
List 5 things you are grateful for.

- _____
- _____
- _____
- _____
- _____

Successes
List 3 things you did well today.

- _____
- _____
- _____

Mindfulness Assignment: Heart Sight
How did it go? What were your preconceived notions/judgments?
Were you able to drop those and see with your heart? What was
that like?

_____

_____

_____

_____

_____

_____

_____

_____

_____

_____

_____

_____

_____

_____

_____

_____

_____

Day 94:

Gratitude List
List 5 things you are grateful for.

- ❖ _____
- ❖ _____
- ❖ _____
- ❖ _____
- ❖ _____

Successes
List 3 things you did well today.

- ❖ _____
- ❖ _____
- ❖ _____

Mindfulness Assignment: Heart Sight
Write about your experiences.

_____

_____

_____

_____

_____

_____

_____

_____

_____

_____

_____

_____

_____

You know the saying "do what you love". Consider this isn't always possible. Life is often mundane and we struggle to find meaning. Let's turn this around and instead "love what you do." Rather than constantly looking for a new path, can you love the path you're on? You've seen how being mindful of ordinary things can bring more heartfulness and gratitude.

Take these tools out into the world and reframe your thoughts in any situation. Look for what you can treasure. See how you have the opportunity to bring your heart forward even as you do the "daily grind."

Day 95: _____

Gratitude List
List 5 things you are grateful for.

- _____
- _____
- _____
- _____
- _____

Successes
List 3 things you did well today.

- _____
- _____
- _____

Mindfulness Assignment: Heart Sight
Write about your experiences.

_____

_____

_____

_____

_____

_____

_____

_____

_____

_____

_____

_____

_____

_____

_____

_____

_____

_____

Day 96: _____

Gratitude List
List 5 things you are grateful for.

- ✍ _____
- ✍ _____
- ✍ _____
- ✍ _____
- ✍ _____

Successes
List 3 things you did well today.

- ✍ _____
- ✍ _____
- ✍ _____

Mindfulness Assignment: Heart Sight
Write about your experiences.

_____

_____

_____

_____

_____

_____

_____

_____

_____

_____

_____

_____

_____

_____

Make a moment!
Take time this week to do something enjoyable, something just for you.

Day 97: _____

Gratitude List
List 5 things you are grateful for.

- _____
- _____
- _____
- _____
- _____

Successes
List 3 things you did well today.

- _____
- _____
- _____

Mindfulness Assignment: Heart Sight
Write about your experiences.

_____
_____
_____
_____
_____
_____
_____
_____
_____

Next Mindfulness Assignment:
Heart Offering
At least once a day, bring your fingers together in front of your heart, fingertips touching pointing away from your heart. Be relaxed, palms not touching. Look into the heart-shaped space created with your hands and breathe. Let what's inside your heart be outside of your body. Offer up your heart to the world.

Day 98:

Gratitude List
List 5 things you are grateful for.

❧ _____

❧ _____

❧ _____

❧ _____

❧ _____

Successes
List 3 things you did well today.

❧ _____

❧ _____

❧ _____

Mindfulness Assignment: Heart Offering
How did the heart offering go? Did you experience a shift in your mood? Your intentions? Were you able to leverage your breath and fingertips to feel your heart?

_____

_____

_____

_____

_____

_____

_____

_____

_____

_____

_____

_____

_____

Reframing reminder
Life can be difficult. I sometimes find myself getting dragged down into a pit of negativity, a place far away from my heart. With reframing, I remember that negative thoughts are normal reactions to being alive and have no real meaning. This helps me detach from them.

Sometimes it's hard to tell if a thought is truly negative, so I ask myself "is this thought helpful?" If it is, I assess how to make it work for me. If it's not helpful, I reframe. There is so much power in knowing I can choose how I process my thoughts.

Day 99: _____

Gratitude List
List 5 things you are grateful for.

- _____
- _____
- _____
- _____
- _____

Successes
List 3 things you did well today.

- _____
- _____
- _____

Mindfulness Assignment: Heart Offering
Write about your experiences.

_____
_____
_____
_____
_____
_____
_____
_____
_____
_____
_____
_____
_____
_____
_____
_____
_____

Day 100: ____________

Gratitude List

List 5 things you are grateful for.

- ____________
- ____________
- ____________
- ____________
- ____________

Successes

List 3 things you did well today.

- ____________
- ____________
- ____________

Mindfulness Assignment: Heart Offering

Write about your experiences.

You have completed
100 days of mindfulness!

Congratulations! You did it! I hope this heart journey has been a fulfilling one.

Be sure to check out the Appendix for ideas for growing your mindfulness practice.

I wish you the very best of everything in life. My heart loves and honors your heart.

NAMASTE

Reflection

What were your favorite mindfulness activities? Have you noticed any change in your heart and attitude? Have there been changes in your relationships?

Which activities did not do much for you? Could those activities provide you with a different experience next time?

Appendix

Growing Your Mindfulness Practice

So where do you go from here? Here are some options to consider.

Yoga – Thousands of years ago, the practice of yoga was created as a way to prepare the mind for meditation. It's sometimes referred to as a "moving meditation." Yoga is amazing, and I have personally experienced a life transformation from the practice. I can't recommend yoga highly enough as a way to get out of your head.

Below are some common venues where you can find yoga:
- Colleges often have beginner yoga classes available to the community for low cost
- Most gyms have yoga classes on their schedules
- Yoga studios usually have classes every day
- Hospitals often have community wellness programs
- The free website Meetup (www.meetup.com) will help you find yoga classes in your area

Meditation – There are a wide variety of meditation styles out there to try. If you're unfamiliar with meditation, I suggest guided meditation where a voice leads you. The availability of guided meditation is tremendous:
- Smartphone apps such as Headspace, Calm, Buddify, Omvana and the Mindfulness App.
- YouTube videos
- iTunes and Amazon Music
- CDs and tapes for purchase on Amazon
- The free website Meetup (www.meetup.com) will help you find meditation sessions in your area
- Yoga studios often have meditation classes too
- Unity Church (www.unity.org) and Unitarian Universalist Church (www.uua.org)
- Buddhist Centers (some meditation sessions can last 1-2 hours, so inquire with them first.)

More Gratitude Ideas

Recalling activities or events from the day can be a source of gratitude. It's just a matter of wording them in a grateful way.

For example, you went to a concert you really enjoyed. You could write, "I am grateful I have the financial means to attend concerts" or "I am grateful for music; it lifts my spirits."

I use my gratitude section to express my gratitude for the things I get to experience, which also serves as a historical record of my life.

Other ideas:

- o Family and friends who support you. List each person individually and what specifically you're grateful for. It could be something they did today.
- o Sunny day, warm day, rainy day
- o Ability to breathe
- o Pets, children, and loved ones showing you they love you. Again, list them individually and what specifically you love about them.
- o Ability to move, walk, exercise, etc.
- o Ability to eat, burp, pass gas, even poop!
- o Eating yummy food.
- o Having a good boss.
- o Having coworkers.
- o Encountering nice smells.
- o Clean water, air conditioning, and heat.
- o Having clothes to wear.
- o Having electronics (TV, phone, computer, tablet, etc.)
- o Music, being able to hear.
- o The sounds of nature.
- o Having shelter.
- o Being able to see colors.
- o Having electricity, the Internet.
- o Seeing art.
- o Being able to read a book.
- o Friends and family.
- o Hearing laughter.
- o Baby animals always make me smile.
- o It can be a fun daily exercise to name one thing you like about a person in your life. You may learn you appreciate much more about them than you realize.

More Successes

Anytime you think of something you did today as not special or too mundane to be a success, shift your thinking. Little accomplishments are still accomplishments.

- o Going to work when you don't feel well
- o Making dinner
- o Eating healthy
- o Sleeping well
- o Getting chores done
- o Getting bills paid
- o Telling someone you love them
- o Enjoying something without being distracted by thoughts

More about "I" Language

Notice in the examples below how I language empowers the speaker.

"You" language: "When you respect and honor and take care of yourself, you are more able to do the same for others."

"I" language: "When I respect and honor and take care of myself, I am more able to do the same for others."

"You" language: "When you practice mindfulness you get more clarity about what you want in life."

"I" language: "My personal experience is that mindfulness has helped me get more clarity about what I want in life."

"You" language: "There are times when you don't stand up for yourself and it makes you feel awful. You don't know if you would stand up next time."

"I" language: "There have been times when I didn't stand up for myself, and it made me feel awful. I am thinking about how to stand up next time."

More about Value-Based Living

The best way I can think of to give more guidance is to provide my own example of using my chosen values to shift my perspective (and hence my mood.)

My values are compassion, generosity, and connection. I remind myself of these values every morning and often think of them during the day. I use these values as guideposts for how I think and react. Some examples of how I use them:

- When I'm in a situation that feels off, my values help me know what to do. I ask myself "is this situation in keeping with my values? Can I change the situation with my actions? Do I need to excuse myself?"

- Gossip is a problem area for me. When I catch myself being part of gossip, I mentally ask: "Am I being compassionate or generous? Is this fostering connection with others?"

- Sometimes my depression makes me want to isolate. I use my value of connection to push myself to go out and be with others (because I know that I really do want connection, it's just my disease getting in the way.)

- For a long time, I was really down on my job. I work for a health insurance company, and it's a big company with lots of cubicles. It's essentially Corporate America. I felt my job wasn't altruistic enough. I wanted to help people. I use my values at work and it has improved my interactions with coworkers. But I started to realize I could take my values-based living to a higher level. Instead of just applying my values to the situation of the moment, I started actively looking for opportunities to exercise my generosity and compassion, to help my coworkers. This led to me becoming a voice for people with mental illness, as well as fighting for the rights of my LGBT coworkers.

Using values to guide my actions helps my anxiety and depression in three ways:

1. It reduces that nagging feeling something is wrong. I believe this feeling comes from disconnect between our values and how we're living our lives. Sometimes we are conscious of this disconnect, but often we aren't and instead know it subconsciously. Either way, the result is unease, which turns into anxiety, and then into depression.

2. Instead of obsessing and stressing over decisions, I bounce the decision against my values to help me decide faster. This way I spend less time under stress. Because I used my values to make my decision, I experience less regret.

3. The many mundane things in my life that used to depress me now have purpose.

It's your turn! Below are some values to get you started:

Accuracy	Faith	Patriotism
Achievement	Family	Perfection
Belonging	Fidelity	Productivity
Cheerfulness	Fitness	Prudence
Commitment	Forgiveness	Quality
Compassion	Freedom	Responsibility
Competitiveness	Fun	Results-
Consistency	Generosity	Oriented
Control	Grace	Safety and
Courage	Growth	Security
Creativity	Hard Work	Self-
Curiosity	Helping Others	Actualization
Dependability	Humility	Self-Control
Devotion	Intellect	Self-Reliance
Diligence	Intelligence	Serenity
Discipline	Justice	Spontaneity
Discretion	Leaving a Legacy	Tolerance
Diversity	Love	Trustworthiness
Education	Loyalty	Truth-Seeking
Efficiency	Making a Difference	Uniqueness
Empathy	Mastery	Usefulness
Enthusiasm	Openness	Vitality
Excellence	Order	
Exploration	Originality	

About the Author

Tracey Moore Lukkarila has worked in the health insurance industry for nearly two decades in a variety of Information Technology, Marketing, and Public Policy roles. She holds a bachelor's degree in Business Administration from the University of North Florida and a masters-level certificate in Public Health from the University of Florida. She is a registered yoga teacher (RYT-200).

Tracey strives to live out her personal values of compassion, generosity, connectedness, and education. She serves as the chair of her employer's Mental Health Collaborative, a peer group that provides support to employees dealing with mental health issues and advises on corporate initiatives to improve employee mental health. She also serves on her employer's lesbian, gay, bisexual, and transgender (LGBT) employee resource group, advocating for LGBT rights in the workplace and statewide. Tracey is very passionate about animals and serves on the board of Friends of Jacksonville Animals (FOJA) and volunteers for the local animal shelter. She loves yoga and teaches the Baptiste Power Yoga methodology in her community. As a lifelong sufferer of anxiety and depression, Tracey aims to bring her professional and personal experiences together to advocate for mental health and to help others who struggle.

Tracey also enjoys arts and crafts, music, film, traveling, hiking, camping, and spending time with friends. She lives with her husband Troy and their five cats and a Chihuahua in Florida.

Visit her blog at www.traceylukkarila.com.